A JOURNEY TO FULLNESS

AN INTRODUCTION
to the Fullness of the Original Christian Faith

16-SESSION WORKBOOK

FATHER BARNABAS POWELL

A Journey to Fullness
is a ministry of
Faith Encouraged Ministries

www.faithencouraged.org

TABLE OF CONTENTS

JESUS ANSWERED AND SAID TO HER, "If you knew the gift of God, and who it is who says to you, 'Give Me a drink,' you would have asked Him, and *He would have given you living water.*"

The woman said to Him, "Sir, You have nothing to draw with, and the well is deep. Where then do You get that living water?"

Jesus answered and said to her, *"Whoever drinks of this water will thirst again, but whoever drinks of the water that I shall give him will never thirst. But the water that I shall give him will become in him a fountain of water springing up into everlasting life."*

JOHN 4:1–14

INTRODUCTION

*"O Savior, who journeyed with Luke and Cleopas to Emmaus,
journey with your servants as they now set out upon their way,
and defend them from all evil."*

—ORTHODOX PRAYER BEFORE BEGINNING A JOURNEY

We are all on a journey. There are times during the journey in which we know precisely where we'd like to go. We know the starting point. We know the roadside attractions, the highway markers and the miles before we reach that destination. But there are other times in which the destination seems unclear. We wander from place to place; we look at maps for inspiration, for illumination, for some clue about what lies ahead.

In the Orthodox tradition, we speak about our lives of faith in this way, referring to our path of Christianity as a journey. Our destination is clear, to be in communion with God, the Maker of All. We navigate this long road with prayer, practice, and community. In building this Orthodox faith, we find the continuity and the care we require to continue along the journey no matter what greets us on the road.

This study is the merest of introductions to the Orthodox faith and the life of the Church. It is hoped that this will help you understand, although in a limited way, what the Eastern Orthodox Church is, and why it holds an attraction for us.

Many Western Christians, on hearing Orthodox doctrines for the first time, are tempted to regard them as either right or wrong. They approach them with the attitude of, "If Orthodoxy is right, then everything I have believed must be wrong!" It is important to understand that this is not the proper way to approach Orthodoxy, with its unfamiliar rhythms and eastern mindset.

First of all, never despise or belittle who you are and what you have been. We are all on a journey. We are growing in grace and learning as we grow. If yours is simply an attempt to get it right, then Orthodoxy may prove to be either overwhelming in its ideas, or you may simply dismiss it with a wave of your hand. In either case, you will be missing out on the riches of Eastern Patristic Christianity.

Secondly, this short study is not meant to convert anyone to Orthodoxy. Conversion is a life-long process and cannot be accomplished in a short time. As you will see in the sessions, Orthodoxy can only be learned with a teacher—a catechist. This short study is simply an introduction to Orthodoxy.

Thirdly, if you should feel pressured at any time during this program, as though someone were expecting you to make some sort of decision to accept or reject Orthodoxy, please understand that it is not our intent to produce such feelings. If you should feel such pressure, just remember this: You are never free to say yes until you are free to say no.

Of course we would like for everyone to become Orthodox. But, it is simply not going to happen. If you learn something about Orthodoxy and decide to neither reject nor accept it, but you simply want to remain friends and continue as you were, we hope that you feel the freedom to do so.

We hope that you will find this series illuminating and life-giving and invite you to enter into the discussions, the further reading and resources, as you feel led.

May the eternal light of God's glory shine on you while you study these things and help you on your journey toward the "goal of your faith, the salvation of your soul." (1 Pet. 1:9.)

Good Journey to you!

—Fr. Barnabas Powell

SESSION 1: *Is This Trip Really Necessary?*

And one called to another and said: "Holy, holy, holy is the Lord of hosts; the whole earth is full of His glory." —ISAIAH 6:3

"The deeper conviction always is that the truth can never be objectified or exhausted, while each human person is also uniquely created in the image of God, never able to be reduced to anything less than a mystery." —ECUMENICAL PATRIARCH BARTHOLOMEW

Overview

If you ask anyone how they came into the Orthodox faith, you are likely to get a variety of answers. No matter the method, the path to Orthodoxy always begins with a discovery of one kind or another. Whether the discovery was long sought after, or simply stumbled across, the fact of discovery is the same. In discovery, we become aware of something new, or at least something unexpected. How we react to this discovery lays the foundation for our experiences going forward.

Father Barnabas tells us in this installment of Journey to Fullness that the purpose of this series is to "explain how the Orthodox faith understands itself." This session, then, is a means to lay the foundation for the series. It bears asking—how does a Pentecostal preacher find his way into Orthodoxy?

For Father Barnabas, finding his way into Orthodoxy begins by a recognition that he is lacking. He discovers that he lacks an in-depth knowledge of church history before the Protestant Reformation, and this weighs upon him. Rather than turning away from that gnawing discovery, he is determined to learn more about those missing pieces. This fuels his curiosity and then leads him to more discoveries—of the historical church, of the church fathers, of Liturgy and of tradition. Each new discovery brings with it a new awareness—a new opportunity for curiosity and learning.

KEY POINTS:

- "Zeal without wisdom is destructive."

  Zeal, as defined by Merriam-Webster, is "an eagerness and ardent interest in pursuit of something." In proper context and with wisdom, "zeal" can be profitable and good.

Without these things, our "zeal" can become an end to itself, causing damage to everyone and everything we touch. Wisdom in the Orthodox tradition is a virtue. It is something to which one aspires, a quality of understanding that is more than simply "knowing" a fact but rather a deep revelation as St. Paul describes in Ephesians: "I do not cease to give thanks for you, remembering you in my prayers, that the God of our Lord Jesus Christ, the Father of glory, may give you a spirit of wisdom and of revelation in the knowledge of Him, having the eyes of your hearts enlightened, that you may know the hope to which He has called you…"

- *"I needed a fireplace for my fire so that the fire of my zeal would be productive and healthy—and not destructive."*

When one thinks about a fireplace, many images may come to mind—river stone, kindling, sturdy wood logs, cozy nights by a fire, comfort. In this metaphor for the Church, we can begin to see the relationship of our zeal (or our fire) as it pertains to the world around us. And in this, we can begin to understand the comfort that the Orthodox tradition offers to those who profess this faith. This "fireplace" of the Orthodox Church is not meant to snuff out the zeal or even to "tame," but rather to help the participant focus his faith and tend that fire in good and healthy ways, ways that will build and benefit.

- *"I finally found a faith that is big enough for the dignity of the human soul."*

The Orthodox faith submits that humankind was created in the image and likeness of God. We are, for all intents and purposes, "icons" of the Creator. St. Gregory Palamas, a noted Orthodox saint and theologian, speaks of the soul in this way: "This image the soul possesses inalienably, even if it does not recognize its own dignity, or think and live in a manner worthy of the Creator's image within it." To find a faith that expresses this dignity, one which the Orthodox believe mirrors the Creator of all things, is a profound statement and a keen discovery.

- *"This journey is about learning how to be so solid, so rooted, so well rounded and whole and healthy that I can pass through my life no matter what I'm facing with the sure knowledge that everything I will ever need is in the hospital of the Orthodox Christian faith."*

When we are confronted on all sides with a culture of change, one that values the "new and improved," this idea that one may find the Orthodox Church sufficient for our needs may seem improbable. But the emphasis here, on being rooted and solid, is important. In order for a tree to grow well, the roots must be healthy. This is the function of the Church for Orthodox Christians, to provide healthy roots and a solid foundation.

Questions for discussion

Consider your own background and experience with church or religion in general. Are there times in which you were spurred in a new direction because of a discovery?

_____

_____

_____

_____

Father Barnabas says when describing his way of understanding faith during his Pentecostal years, "It was just the language I knew." If you were to describe your "language" for understanding faith, what would it be?

_____

_____

_____

How important to you is "history" when considering matters of faith?

_____

_____

_____

SESSION 2: *What is the Orthodox Church?*

When the Day of Pentecost had fully come, they were all with one accord in one place. And suddenly there came a sound from heaven, as of a rushing mighty wind, and it filled the whole house where they were sitting. Then there appeared to them divided tongues, as of fire, and one sat upon each of them. And they were all filled with the Holy Spirit and began to speak with other tongues, as the Spirit gave them utterance. —ACTS 2:1–4

"For one thing it would take a long while: my name is growing all the time, and I've lived a very long, long time; so my name is like a story. Real names tell you the story of things they belong to in my language, in the Old Entish as you might say. It is a lovely language, but it takes a very long time saying anything in it, because we do not say anything in it, unless it is worth taking a long time to say, and to listen to." —TREEBEARD, The Two Towers, by J.R.R. Tolkien

Overview

It seems, at first glance, to be a simple enough question, "What is the Orthodox Church?" But, like many aspects of Orthodoxy, the answer unfolds with a complex, beautiful, and rich answer. The eastern mindset in which the Orthodox Church has been formed, historically, ensures this. This way of understanding questions like this shows that the Church takes the answers quite seriously.

In order to gain insights into the Orthodox tradition, we go back to the start of Orthodoxy, on the day of Pentecost. The Church begins on this day with the Apostles' receipt of the gifts of the Holy Spirit in the upper room. The early Church grew and developed for over a thousand years until the Great Schism of 1054. The "western" church, or the Roman church, led by the Roman Patriarch of that time, split from the traditional Orthodox faith. This Roman Church became what is known today as the Roman Catholic Church and that Roman Patriarch continues as the leader of the faith as the Pope.

At its core, the Orthodox faith can best be described by its very name: *Ortho,* meaning right or correct, and *Doxa,* meaning worship or glory. The name Orthodox, right worship or right glory, reveals the Church as being defined by the way we worship.

The Orthodox faith continues to this day with the same conviction that began in A.D. 33 in that upper room with the gift of the Holy Spirit. Though the ethnic flavors of Orthodoxy may differ slightly—Greek, Antiochian, Serbian, Russian—the essence and practice of Orthodoxy is the same, all seeking to aspire to the fullness of God, in correct doctrine, right worship.

KEY QUOTES:

- *"The interesting thing about the Orthodox faith is that you begin to understand that it is that timelessness and the continuity that is part of the revelation of what the Orthodox faith is all about."*

The Orthodox Liturgy is conducted around the world in much the same way regardless of location. The Divine Liturgy had its origins in the early Church. It was first described by Justin the Martyr in A.D. 138, then grew and developed over the course of many years. The current version *(in particular, the Divine Liturgy of St. John Chrysostom)* has been celebrated in the Orthodox Church in some form since the early fifth century.

- *"One of the very first keys is the word Orthodox itself. It comes from two Greek words, ortho and doxa—which literally means correct or right glory, or correct or right worship, or correct or right doctrine. It's about being full. It's about being complete. "*

When describing the Orthodox faith, you may hear this term, "full" or "fullness" used quite a bit. Orthodox priest and author Father Stephen Freeman uses this explanation, "I prefer to use the term 'fullness' when describing the Orthodox faith because it is far more explanatory than simply saying that we are the 'true Church,' etc. 'Fullness,' of course, does not deny this, but it moves us onto more fruitful ground."

- *"The Orthodox Church understands herself as the body of Christ."*

When we speak of the "body of Christ" it's helpful to keep in mind the words of St. Paul in the book of Romans, "For as we have many members in one body, but all the members do not have the same function, so we, being many, are one body in Christ, and individually members of one another." In this way we see that the life and vibrancy of the Church. This is an important aspect of the Orthodox tradition.

- *"When we say the Orthodox Church, we mean the Church of the seven councils, we mean the Church of the Holy Fathers, we mean the Church of Pentecost, we mean the Orthodox Christian Church."*

Returning to the theme of timelessness and continuity, we remember once again that the Orthodox Church has deep roots, and a long tradition that began with the gift of the Holy Spirit to the Apostles and continues until this very day.

Questions for discussion

What was your first introduction to Orthodox Christianity? How did you first hear of it?

_____

_____

_____

_____

The words *correct* or *right* can bring with them some degree of baggage. What does this concept bring up for you as you hear it in this context?

_____

_____

_____

_____

When you consider the unchanging nature of Orthodoxy and the two-thousand-year history of it, what comes to mind? In a culture driven by "change" is there some advantage to this approach?

_____

_____

_____

_____

_____

SESSION 3: *When Did Orthodoxy Begin?*

"But this I confess to you, that according to the Way which they call a sect, so I worship the God of my fathers, believing all things which are written in the Law and in the Prophets."
—ACTS 24:14

"Apart from love nothing whatever has existed, nor ever will. Its names and actions are many. More numerous still are its distinctive marks; divine and innumerable are its properties. Yet it is one in nature, wholly beyond utterance whether on the part of angels or men or any other creatures, even such as are unknown to us. Reason cannot comprehend it; its glory is inaccessible, its counsels unsearchable. It is eternal because it is beyond time, invisible because thought cannot comprehend it, though it may perceive it. Many are the beauties of this holy Sion not made with hands! He who has begun to see it no longer delights in sensible objects; he ceases to be attached to the glory of this world." —ST. SYMEON THE NEW THEOLOGIAN

Overview

In order to understand new concepts, it's important to know our starting point, and at the same time be able to set aside our preconceived notions. Knowing how we are formed (our own history and our own mindset) helps us to keep an open view of these new concepts.

This means that we must be willing to take a step back so that we can look at the larger picture before us, taking into account all of history, and perhaps seeing things from a different perspective. In examining and understanding the great tradition of Orthodoxy, we return to its roots and look at the condition of the world into which the figure of Christ was born, and see too how the timing of His coming was important.

When we step back to see that larger picture, we discover when we return to the start of the Orthodox faith that the Orthodox Church is rooted in an *eastern* mindset. The Eastern Orthodox Church is still, in fact, *eastern* in its thinking. This eastern mindset comes from the continuity of the Old Testament, and the Hebrew tradition in which the early Christians were formed. The timing of the start of the Orthodox Church is significant. The result of that timing is a combination of the Hebrew tradition with the strong philosophical bend in the Hellenic mindset of that time. This is most evident in the Divine Liturgy but it is the underpinning of the faith and shows itself throughout the history of the Church.

KEY POINTS:

- *"The earliest Christians were shaped by 6,000 years of Hebrew thinking and the Hebrew way of doing things. That Hebrew mindset was very intimate with God and very intimate with the Creator."*

The accounts in the creation story of Genesis show this concept beautifully—in the way God *breathes* life into the clay-formed Adam, that He creates man in His "own image" and in the way He searches for Adam and Eve after they sample the fruit of the forbidden tree. Even in the most difficult passages of the Old Testament, the relationship with God is intimate and tangible.

- *"The people heard the Scriptures in the context of the Orthodox Christian liturgy."*

The Divine Liturgy that we practice in the Orthodox Church each week is built upon the reading of Scriptures. It is the foundation of the worship. Fr. John Breck says in his essay on Bible and Liturgy: "A defining characteristic of Orthodox Christianity is the intimate and inseparable relationship it preserves between Bible and Liturgy, between divine revelation as the canonical or normative source of our faith, and celebration of that faith in the worship of the Church. Faith, grounded in Scripture, determines the content of our worship; worship gives expression to our faith."

- *"The mindset of the Orthodox Faith is decidedly Hellenic and Semitic."*

Modern philosopher William Barrett describes in further detail the differences in the eastern (Hebrew) and western (Hellenic) mindsets: "The distinction . . . arises from the difference between doing and knowing. The Hebrew is concerned with practice, the Greek with knowledge. Right conduct is the ultimate concern of the Hebrew, right thinking that of the Greek. Duty and strictness of conscience are the paramount things in life for the Hebrew; for the Greek, the spontaneous and luminous play of the intelligence. The Hebrew thus extols the moral virtues as the substance and meaning of life; the Greek subordinates them to the intellectual virtues . . . the contrast is between practice and theory, between the moral man and the theoretical or intellectual man." In this way we begin to see, once again, that the posture of the Orthodox faith is one of fullness."

Questions for discussion

The word *consistent* is a recurring theme so far in this series about Orthodoxy. When you think about what you've heard so far in the program, where do you see that consistency?

_____

_____

_____

_____

If you were to talk about your own "mindset" as it pertains to the way you view the world, how would you describe it?

_____

_____

_____

_____

Is the concept of "liturgy" familiar to you already? What is your perception of this idea of "liturgy?"

_____

_____

_____

_____

SESSION 4: *Characteristics of Orthodox Christianity*

"Therefore take heed to yourselves and to all the flock, among which the Holy Spirit has made you overseers, to shepherd the church of God which He purchased with His own blood.
—Acts 20:28

"The Church of Christ is One, Holy, Universal and Apostolic. She is herself a single spiritual body, whose head is Christ, and who has the one Holy Spirit abiding in her. The local parts of the Church are members of a single body of the Universal Church, and they, like branches of a single tree, are nourished by one and same sap from a single root. She is called holy because she is sanctified by the holy word, deeds, sacrifice and suffering of her founder, Jesus Christ, to which end He came in order to save human beings and lead them to holiness. The Church is called universal because she is not confined by place, not by time, nor by nation nor language. The Church communicates with all humanity. The Orthodox Church is called apostolic because the spirit, teaching and labors of the Apostles of Christ are entirely preserved in her."
—St. Nicholas of Serbia, *Catechesis*

Overview

The way the Orthodox church describes or understands herself breaks down into four main characteristics—One, Holy, Catholic and Apostolic. Each of these words carries with it a distinct historical and theological meaning. Just as we see when we use the words Orthodox, Amen or Alleluia, we simply transliterate the words so that we do not misunderstand the meaning as it pertains to the tradition.

When we say, as Orthodox Christians, the Church is "One," we mean the Church cannot be denominated. It cannot be broken apart. When we say the Church is one, we mean that the unity of the Church cannot be changed. It cannot be minimized and cannot be destroyed by time, by distance, by death, or anything else.

The word "Holy" in regard to the Orthodox Church literally means "set apart for a specific use." If something is *holy,* as we understand the Church is holy, we mean that the Church belongs exclusively to Jesus Christ. The Church exists for one purpose and one purpose only, and that is to be the body of Christ in the Earth to continue the ministry of Christ on the Earth.

The word "Catholic" comes from the Greek word *catholicos,* which means literally, "according to the whole." When the Orthodox Church says we believe that we are a Catholic Church, it means that we understand the Church is whole. It's complete. It's well rounded. It's mature. It's grown-up. It has everything you need.

The word "Apostolic" means that this Church, the Orthodox Church, is the continuity of the teaching of the apostles to this very day. But this continuity is more than simply preserving a kind of "dogma" initiated in the first century. To follow the Apostolic leading is to perpetuate the *experience* of the apostles. The Orthodox Church of today, being rooted in the apostolic tradition, continues to teach exactly what the apostles taught when Christianity began and to share in this same, intimate experience of God.

KEY POINTS:

- *"The original word church is* ekklesia, *'the gathering.'"*

  The word "ekklesia" appears in the New Testament over one hundred times, describing these assemblies or gatherings of the believers and teachers of the rapidly growing Christian faith.

- *"It's the unity of the Church that gives credibility to the message of the Church and the lack of unity of the Church takes away credibility from the message of the Church."*

  The apparent splintering of the Christian faith began first with the schism of the Western Church (Roman Catholic) from the Eastern Church (Orthodox). Since that time, and more particularly since the 16th century and the Protestant Reformation, over 33,000 "denominations" have developed. Eastern Orthodoxy has remained "one" Church.

- *"The Church understands herself as one, she understands herself as holy, she understands herself as Catholic, and she understands herself as apostolic."*

  These four qualities or characteristics of the Orthodox Church are foundational. They are the underpinning of all the Orthodox doctrine. Keeping these in mind as the program continues will help to add context to the content.

- *"The Church, because of her oneness, keeps continuity with the teaching of the apostles up to this moment. It isn't that it's old, it's that it's timeless."*

"Timelessness" and "continuity" are key terms when discussing the Orthodox Church. That the tradition exists and continues with vibrancy after two thousand years is significant.

Questions for discussion

When we talk about things as *timeless* or *continuous*, what images come to mind from our modern, daily lives?

_____

_____

_____

_____

The idea that a tradition can offer continuity in a constantly changing culture can seem counter-intuitive to our modern thinking. What is striking to you about this concept of continuity as it pertains to Orthodoxy?

_____

_____

_____

_____

If there were stumbling points for you with any of the four words used here— One, Holy, Catholic and Apostolic—what would they be?

_____

_____

SESSION 5: *Mindset Matters*

"Grace and peace be multiplied to you in the knowledge of God and of Jesus our Lord, as His divine power has given to us all things that pertain to life and godliness, through the knowledge of Him who called us by glory and virtue, by which have been given to us exceedingly great and precious promises, that through these you may be partakers of the divine nature."
—2 PETER 1:2–4

"No matter how much we may study, it is not possible to come to know God unless we live according to His commandments, for God is not known by science, but by the Holy Spirit. Many philosophers and learned men came to the belief that God exists, but they did not know God. It is one thing to believe that God exists and another to know Him. If someone has come to know God by the Holy Spirit, his soul will burn with love for God day and night, and his soul cannot be bound to any earthly thing." —ST. SILOUAN THE ATHONITE, *Writings, VIII.3*

Overview

Continuing with the examination of the Orthodox "mindset," there are four basic "attitudes" that the Church exhibits. These attitudes shape the understanding of the faith. The Orthodox tradition approaches matters of faith as communal, intuitive, holistic and mystical.

Communal, as it applies to the Orthodox Church, means that the Church sees herself as a healthy, integrated family—loving and welcoming.

The *intuitive* quality of the Orthodox Church means that we are more than merely analytical or rational. We take into account the full spectrum of experience—intellectual, spiritual, and emotional.

The word *holistic* takes its root from the Greek, *holos,* meaning "whole." The Orthodox Church takes the attitude that the faith is "whole" of what is needed to navigate the highs and lows of life. It provides the tools necessary to become the person we have been created to become. In other words, I can become who I *really* am.

Mystical, from the Greek "mysterion," moves away from the modern notion of finding "solutions," as one might be inclined when thinking of a "mystery." Instead we embrace the concept of mystery being a theology so big that we can never fully exhaust our pursuit of it.

KEY POINTS:

- *"As we talk about the challenge that Orthodoxy presents to our western way of thinking: our western way of thinking is very analytical; our western way of thinking is very much 'let's take it apart and see how it works.'"*

Though the "analytical" or "western" mindset has been in practice for centuries, it is the hallmark of modern life. This approach can feel more productive and therefore more valuable in our current culture.

- *"The eastern mindset says 'let's step back and watch it and see how it acts.' With that kind of eastern mindset that means that I am going to not try to take something apart, I'm going to try to observe and learn."*

To choose the eastern mindset, in this respect, is an act of trust and an exercise in patience. This can tend to run counter to our typical, particularly American, way of behaving.

- *"The Orthodox Christian faith, developing as it did throughout the centuries, understands that the Christian faith is meant to be lived and experienced—not merely reduced to rules and regulations."*

The role of rules or regulations in our daily lives is clear. Without the rules and regulations we may be thrown into chaos. Rules and regulations help us to be productive and healthy members of society.

- *"If the Church understands herself as communal, intuitive, holistic, and mystical, she incorporates all of what it means to be a human person created in the image of God to become in His likeness. That's the purpose of the Orthodox faith."*

The Orthodox Church, in this way, once again shows itself as the "fullness" or the "wholeness" in its approach to faith. This is a departure from our current cultural preference of taking things apart, parsing knowledge and sub-contracting out our lives to specialists.

Questions for discussion

Does your approach to new concepts lean more toward the "analytical" or the "intuitive" side? If there were roadblocks to seeing things in this "intuitive" way, what would they be?

_____

_____

_____

_____

The decision to observe (intuitive, or eastern thought) rather than act (analytical or western thought) is a commitment that requires patience. Where do you see this tension in your own experience?

_____

_____

_____

_____

Can you think of another concept you've encountered that required this experiential approach, something you could not truly understand without experiencing?

_____

_____

_____

Session 6: *A Healing Purpose*

"For whatever was written in earlier times was written for our instruction, so that through perseverance and the encouragement of the Scriptures we might have hope. Now may the God who gives perseverance and encouragement grant you to be of the same mind with one another according to Christ Jesus, so that with one accord you may with one voice glorify the God and Father of our Lord Jesus Christ." —ROMANS 15:4–6

"The chief end of our life is to live in communion with God. To this end the Son of God became incarnate, in order to return us to this divine communion, which was lost by the fall into sin. Through Jesus Christ, the Son of God, we enter into communion with the Father and thus attain our purpose." —ST. THEOPHAN THE RECLUSE

Overview

The popular view of the notions of sin and salvation, predominantly in Protestant theology, is that the sacrifice of Christ was a payment for our original sin. The Orthodox faith understands these concepts differently. Original sin as described in the book of Genesis is about relationship between God and man, newly created in His image. The choice made by man in the story of Adam and Eve in the garden is one that breaks the budding relationship. In the Orthodox understanding, the goal from here forward is always about rebuilding that relationship—not punishment or anger, but redemption.

When we talk about this term in Orthodoxy, we understand it to mean that sin is the wounding of a relationship that is meant to be healed. In this way we see that "sin" is not a breaking of arbitrary rules, but rather, engaging in attitudes, acts, or beliefs that ultimately cause or continue the disruption of a strong, healthy, mature relationship with the Creator.

Salvation, then, as the Orthodox understand it, means that we are saved to a loving relationship with God. We are put back on the right path to build the relationship and encourage a deeper knowledge of God.

KEY POINTS:

- *"To reduce the idea of sin to the breaking of a rule is too small."*

  A simple but powerful analogy is to see this in a parent/child relationship. When we think of the acts of a healthy and mature parent who sets rules, we see that this set of rules is meant to offer protection for a child until they are ready to choose for themselves. The danger in breaking the rules is to the child, the protection is compromised, and the trust between parent and child is tested.

- *"The understanding in the Orthodox Church of sin isn't the breaking of a rule, but the wounding of a relationship, the wounding and the marring of the image of God that we are all created in. We are all created in the image of God, according to the Christian faith."*

For most Western theologians, sin came to mean an insult to God's dignity, and salvation came to mean the dealing with mankind's breaking of God's commandments. Whereas, in the East, sin was viewed as a wounding of the original image in mankind, and a breaking of the relationship between God and mankind. Salvation, for Orthodoxy, means restoring the relationship and the fellowship between God and man, restoring the image to wholeness. It also means theosis—mankind becoming like God.

- *"God sent Adam and Eve out of the garden to protect them, not because He's angry with them, not because He's upset with them. God sends them out of the garden out of an act of love for them."*

This act of love is a protective posture, giving mankind the time and space necessary to heal what is now broken as a result of turning away from God. It is not a punitive measure but a preserving measure.

- *"I get to restore my relationship with Jesus Christ and God the Father. I get to have that healed so that I can become what I was always meant to become, God's eternal companion, who loves me and has given Himself for me. That's the Orthodox faith."*

The Orthodox perception of the concept of salvation and the effect of the occasion of sin are presented as opportunities for growth, health, maturity, and peace.

Questions for discussion

When you hear the words "sin" and "salvation" what comes to mind? How did these ideas or these concepts form?

_____

_____

_____

_____

If we view the story of the Garden of Eden in the way the Orthodox view it, does it change your perception of that story? If so, how?

_____

_____

_____

_____

Is hearing that the Orthodox view of salvation is about healing a relationship with God a new concept for you? What are your thoughts about this view?

_____

_____

_____

Session 7: *Truth and Tradition*

"Now I praise you because you remember me in everything and hold firmly to the traditions, just as I delivered them to you." —1 CORINTHIANS 11:1–2

"Truth is not a thought, not a word, not a relationship between things, not a law. Truth is a Person. It is a Being, which exceeds all beings and gives life to all. If you seek truth with love and for the sake of love, she will reveal the light of His face to you inasmuch as you are able to bear it without being burned. —ST. NICHOLAS OF SERBIA, *Thoughts on Good and Evil*

Overview

Truth and tradition are hot-button issues among Christian faiths. In the Orthodox Church, tradition plays a significant role in the faith of her believers. The eastern mindset, once again, approaches these concepts very differently from the western mindset. The Great Schism in 1054 between Rome and the Orthodox Church began the fracturing of that tradition. The Protestant Reformation and the subsequent movement of Christianity further away from that eastern mindset brought about a further separation from the notion of tradition.

Tradition, in the Orthodox Church, however, is foundational in that it represents the continuity represented in our history together. Tradition is sacred and this tradition is followed not because of rules and regulations or "precepts" but because of the familial nature of the Church. It is this family that helps us to keep our bearings and remain accountable to one another.

In this way, truth, too, can sometimes take on a convoluted pallor when separated from its scriptural and familial context. Taken apart from the knowledge that truth and tradition are rooted in community, and Church as family, these ideas are unmoored, shifting and suspect. The Orthodox Church returns again and again to tradition and truth as ways of knowing that do not shift, but maintain a healthy, mature continuity and consistency.

KEY POINTS:

- *"If you're a too small believer it isn't that you're bad or wrong or ignorant, it's that what you should be is not obtainable to you because you're making final decisions about important things without all the information."*

Here, we reiterate a main theme for this series—challenging our perceptions and expanding our understanding so that we can gain wisdom we did not know we were lacking when we began.

- *"We understand the Holy Scriptures as part of our sacred tradition, in fact all other traditions flow from the traditional understanding of the Holy Scriptures."*

Sola scriptura comes from the Latin, meaning "by scripture alone." It is the belief that the Bible is the supreme authority in all matters of doctrine and practice. This concept arose from the Protestant reformation in response to what was perceived as an over-reliance on tradition by the Roman Catholic Church at that time. While *Sola scriptura* does not deny that other authorities govern Christian life and devotion, it does view them as subordinate to, and corrected by, the written word of God.

- *"The tradition of the faith is called sacred tradition. Now in the West, especially after the West lost the balancing aspects of the Eastern part of the faith, the West began to develop an attitude toward tradition that was very much legalistic."*

As the Christian Church moved further from the historical eastern mindset, which was, as we remember, holistic and intuitive in nature, this attitude of "taking apart" aspects of the Christian life became more prevalent. This is why the Orthodox Church always seeks to embody the "fullness" of the faith, embracing tradition and scripture in a balanced and whole approach.

- *"The Bible doesn't testify to a set of precepts, the Bible testifies to a Person."*

In the book of John, the words of Christ show this testimony clearly— "Jesus said to him, 'I am the way, the truth, and the life. No one comes to the Father except through Me.'" This one verse on its own is extraordinary in that it encapsulates the Orthodox perspective without limiting it.

Questions for discussion

When you consider the word "tradition" what does it bring to mind? Family? Faith? Heritage?

_____

_____

_____

_____

When we talk about seeking or knowing "truth," what does this bring to mind? How do you define this in your own life?

_____

_____

_____

_____

How does the Orthodox view of these concepts square with your experience?

_____

_____

_____

_____

Session 8: *How Do I Understand the Bible?*

"Now the apostles and elders came together to consider this matter. And when there had been much dispute, Peter rose up and said to them: 'Men and brethren, you know that a good while ago God chose among us, that by my mouth the Gentiles should hear the word of the gospel and believe. So God, who knows the heart, acknowledged them by giving them the Holy Spirit, just as He did to us, and made no distinction between us and them, purifying their hearts by faith.'" —ACTS 15:6–9

"In all things that you find in the Holy Scriptures, seek out the purpose of the words, that you may enter into the depth of the thoughts of the saints and understand them with greater exactness. Do not approach the reading of the Divine Scriptures without prayer and asking the help of God. Consider prayer to be the key to the true understanding of that which is said in the Holy Scriptures." —ST. ISAAC THE SYRIAN

Overview

The Orthodox view of the Bible, the Holy Scriptures, flows from how the Church understands herself, which is One (unified), Holy (holistic), Catholic (whole) and Apostolic (continuous). The role of Holy Scriptures in the Orthodox Church is integrated fully with its tradition and history. The Church approaches the understanding of the Bible with three criteria—Universality, Antiquity and Consensus.

To understand Scripture within the criteria of *Universality,* we return to the belief that the Orthodox Church understands herself as "whole" or undivided. What is believed by the larger Church, absent boundaries or borders?

Applying the criteria of *Antiquity* when reading and interpreting scripture we look to the historical understanding according to the writing of the Holy Fathers and saints and the discussions held during the Councils. What is the consistent view throughout centuries?

Consensus arises from tradition, wisdom, discussion, and agreement, and is best seen evidenced in Church history from the Seven Ecumenical Councils that occurred in the first thousand years from the start of the Orthodox Church.

KEY POINTS:

- *"Holy Tradition includes the Holy Scriptures, the Holy Scriptures are the pinnacle of sacred, or holy tradition. It's the top of holy tradition, in fact all Holy Tradition flows from the Holy Tradition preserved in the Holy Scriptures."*

In Orthodoxy, the Bible does not stand alone, outside all other sources of revelation, as an infallible guide to truth. Rather, the Bible is seen as part of the truth handed down by Christ to the apostles, and by the apostles to faithful Christians. The Orthodox call this Sacred Tradition.

- *"And so what is the specific use that the scriptures are set apart for? The Holy Scriptures are holy because the Holy Scriptures give us an accurate record of the work of the Holy Spirit in the midst of His family; the Church."*

In Sacred Tradition, a unique pre-eminence belongs to the Bible, to the Nicene Creed, and to the Seven Ecumenical Councils. Orthodox Christians believe these are absolute and unchanging.

- *"St. Vincent in his book called* A Commonitory *said that the best way to remain safe in your understanding of the Holy Scriptures is to believe what has been believed everywhere, always, and by all."*

St. Vincent of Lerins, a little-known monk, wrote a treatise called *A Commonitory* ("An Aid to Remembering") in about A.D. 434. More clearly than anyone, St. Vincent establishes the tests for determining biblical interpretation.

- *"So our attitude towards the Holy Scriptures is wisdom. This isn't legislation, this isn't 'if you break the rules God's going to mark it down in His book and all forbearance for you.' That's not the way God does things, and it's not the way the Orthodox Church operates."*

When it comes to interpreting the Scriptures, we must be careful that our interpretation of it agrees with what has been spoken by the Holy Spirit through all the ages. There are "tests" that we may use to determine whether something is true, or whether it agrees with truth. One should not simply proclaim "private" interpretations of Scripture, ignoring nearly 20 centuries of consistent Christian Tradition—many times witnessed by millions of ultimate sacrifices—that of martyrdom. (RTB pg 27)

Questions for discussion

When we talk about "remaining safe" in understanding scripture, what does this say to you?

_____

_____

_____

_____

The modern culture has a love-hate relationship with "new and improved." We want something that will be more efficient and deliver benefit but we also pine for roots, history, and tradition. Do you see this tension evidenced in daily life?

_____

_____

_____

_____

To say, as the Orthodox Church believes, that we can only understand Scripture in community is a bold statement in a culture that pushes individuality. How does this approach strike you?

_____

_____

_____

_____

Session 9: *When We Say God, Part 1*

> *"Go therefore and make disciples of all the nations, baptizing them in the name of the Father and of the Son and of the Holy Spirit, teaching them to observe all things that I have commanded you."* —MATTHEW 28:19–20

> *"The person advancing in the spiritual life studies three things: the commandments, doctrine, and faith in the Holy Trinity."* —ST. THALASSIOS THE LIBYAN, "On Love, Self-Control and Life in Accordance with the Intellect," 3.28, *The Philokalia: The Complete Text (Vol. 2)*

Overview

The Orthodox answer to the question, "Who is God?" begins with an explanation of the Holy Trinity. We believe in a God in "three persons"—God the Father, the creator of all things; God the Son in the person of Jesus Christ; and God the Holy Spirit, the wonderful counselor sent to the disciples at the Pentecost.

In this answer, we return to the realm of *mystery* as the Orthodox view it. For a real understanding of the Trinity, we must be willing to put aside our Western mindset, once again, suppressing our automatic tendency to "take apart" the concept in favor of embracing that we cannot ever fully comprehend.

In pondering the Holy Trinity, we recognize that we are confronted with the shortcomings of our rational abilities. We cannot truly adore a God that we can completely understand. This is the Orthodox view of God, intimate and immense at the same time.

KEY POINTS:

- *"The doctrine of the Holy Trinity is absolutely essential to the understanding of the Orthodox Christian faith. . . . For instance, when I talk about the Holy Trinity, I want you to know that the faith clearly teaches that we believe in one God. In fact, the creed that we say in every worship service says, "I believe in one God, the Father." That's how we begin the creed of the ancient Church, of the timeless Church."*

  The Orthodox believe that your view of the Holy Trinity shapes your worship, your view of Christ, your relationship with your spouse and children, your boss, your co-workers, how you think the Church should be governed, your view of what

41

salvation is, how you vote, how you live, and how you die. Your view of the Holy Trinity will affect every aspect of your life.

- *"God has given eternal life to the whole human race. The only issue to be settled is, will you know how to enjoy it? That's what the faith is all about. The foundation of learning how to enjoy eternity is the contemplation, and the living out, and the grasping of, and the pressing through, the concept of the Holy Trinity. God is one God in three persons."*

We return to the idea of mindset here, accessing this eastern understanding once again, in order to comprehend the deeper ideas present. We must move outside of "reason" so that we see things anew. As we hear in Romans 12:2, we are then transformed by the renewing of our minds. The ability to move away from reason and toward the mystery requires trust, and a desire to move toward communion with God, our creator and sustainer.

- *"When the Orthodox Church uses the word 'mystery', we are speaking very specifically, not about a puzzle to be solved, but about a truth so big that no matter how much I learn about it, I will never exhaust it. There will always be more to learn."*

The glorious mystery of the Holy Trinity is that out of, and based on His love, the Father eternally begets the Son, and, from the same Father, the Spirit eternally proceeds. Each divine person fully sharing, in equal measure, the one divine nature, but expressing that divine nature in a free, unique, and unrepeatable way.

- *"The Church in her wisdom and God in His infinite vastness gives us the revelation of the Holy Trinity to crucify our intellect and to give us an opportunity to learn what it means to repent—not to say I'm sorry for breaking the rules, but to come to the end of myself where I come and learn how to adore God."*

This Great Mystery forces prideful man to repent (to change his mind). We are called, when confronted with this Great Mystery, to change our minds, change our habitual ways of thinking, and be converted.

Questions for discussion

What do *you* mean when you say the word "God"?

_____

_____

_____

_____

Does this Orthodox understanding of "mystery" have any parallels in your current thinking?

_____

_____

_____

_____

What has been your historical perception of the concept of the Holy Trinity?

_____

_____

_____

_____

Session 10: *When We Say God, Part 2*

"That they may be one, even as We are One." —John 17:22

"As the Holy Trinity, our God is One Being, although Three Persons, so, likewise, we ourselves must be one. As our God is indivisible, we also must be indivisible, as though we were one man, one mind, one will, one heart, one goodness, without the smallest admixture of malice—in a word, one pure love, as God is Love." —St. John of Kronstadt

Overview

The theology of the Trinity, while a mystery, is also a guiding template for the whole of the Orthodox Faith. We see this theme echo throughout the practices of Orthodoxy. We see it in the prayerful repetition of "holy, holy, holy" in the Divine Liturgy, and the daily prayers of her people. We see it even in the design of the church building itself—the Narthex, the Nave, and the Holy of Holies, three separate parts of the same church building.

The way we speak of God as three "persons" rather than "individuals" is important. This terminology reveals a need for the presence of community. Relationship is at the heart of the Orthodox Faith. God made us to be in communion with one another because He, Himself, is in communion at His very essence.

KEY POINTS:

- *"God and His love for us reveal to us the mystery of the Holy Trinity as a unique and spiritual gift for we humans. In the Christian faith, the Orthodox Christian faith, this gift is given to us specifically to make us able to enjoy God forever."*

  Remember that our goal isn't to convince you that Orthodoxy is right, or the best way. Our goal is to know God better and love Him more, so that we can continually be brought into a deeper relationship with Him. Our goal is to fully embrace all the teachings of the Church on this foundational truth.

- *"The common divine nature is personified in each person of the Holy Trinity in a free, unique, and unrepeatable way, just like you and me."*

  Orthodox theologian and author Christos Yannaras describes this in detail in his book

The Freedom of Morality (NY: SVS Press, 1984). "Each person is a sum of characteristics common to all human nature, to mankind as a whole, and at the same time he transcends it inasmuch as he is an existential distinctiveness, a fact of existence which cannot be defined objectively."

- *"It is the overcoming of the brokenness of creation that is at the heart of the spiritual medicine of the Orthodox Christian faith. That's because of our unique understanding of the doctrine of the Holy Trinity. That's why it's the foundation of all Orthodox worship, prayer, and work."*

The Scripture tells us over and over again that it is to the Father that Christ longs to reconcile us and that ultimately it is to the Father that all things will be offered up. Christ will one day offer up the Kingdom to the Father at the end of all things. So history is moving toward a certain end.

The idea of the Church as a hospital shows itself in early writings of the Church and is a guiding point in the doctrine. One of the earliest and most noteworthy references would be this quote from St. John Chrysostom: "Enter into the Church and wash away your sins. For here there is a hospital and not a court of law."

- *"God knows Himself as persons in communion. That word there, 'persons,' is significant because person is not the same as individual. That's the reason why I can say there is one God. A person is not an individual. An individual can be by himself, but a person to be a real person must be in communion."*

The ministry of Christ is to bring reconciliation. First of all, reconciling us to the Father, and secondly, reconciling us to each other. This brings us to the Person of the Holy Spirit.

Questions for discussion

When you consider the differentiation here between person and individual, what comes to mind?

_____

_____

_____

_____

What role has "relationship" played in your previous experience with matters of faith?

_____

_____

_____

_____

If there has been something that you have been surprised to learn so far in this series, what has it been?

_____

_____

_____

_____

Session 11: *God With Us*

"For God so loved the world that He gave His only begotten Son, that whoever believes in Him should not perish but have everlasting life." —JOHN 3:16

"The flood of temporal things draws us after itself, but in this flood there is, as it were, a full grown tree: our Lord Jesus Christ. He took flesh, died, and ascended to heaven. It is as if He agreed to be in the flood of the temporal. Is this stream dragging you headlong? Hold on to Christ." —ST. AUGUSTINE

Overview

We have heard now about the doctrine of the Holy Trinity as foundational to the Orthodox Church. The doctrine helps to inform all of the elements of the Orthodox faith, tradition, and practice. This is an essential part of understanding the roots of the Church as well as the current-day practices.

The doctrine of the Trinity is foundational because we are created in God's image, to be made into His likeness. This element of the doctrine is eminently practical, in fact, because through this revelation, we come to know ourselves. We are invited to enter into the eternal communion of the Father, Son, and Holy Spirit.

The Orthodox style of worship is sensory: heavy on the incense, the imagery, the sign of the cross, prostrations, prayers, and iconography. In all of these things we are making "visible the invisible." Our model for this is, of course, Christ, the Son of God who took on flesh to live and dwell among us. He is "God with us."

The degree of physicality with which the Orthodox Church approaches not only worship, but also prayer practices, life in community, and relationship with God, has in mind the ultimate goal of restoration. The reality of God with us, in the person of Jesus, points the way toward that restoration and makes it possible.

KEY POINTS:

- *"If you begin to appreciate the nuances and the beauty of God revealing His inner life to us, specifically for our good, then you'll begin to understand why God does what He does."*

It is in this infused goodness of creation that the Christian rejoices. It is also the reason St. Paul says that even creation groans for the manifestation of the children of God (Romans 8:18–21). Why? Because when all things are summed up in Christ on the last day, then, and only then, will creation be completely liberated to do what it was created to do: Reflect God's Glory! Dostoevsky has said, "Beauty will save the world." Orthodoxy is the embodiment of this idea.

- *"Jesus comes in the flesh so that the flesh that had been corrupted by sin and death and selfishness could be restored to being what it was meant to be in the first place, and that was to be a bearer of the goodness of God."*

Ultimate truth, for Orthodox Christians, is not a doctrine or belief—it is a person, the Lord Jesus Christ. This quote from Mother Maria of Normandy states it best: "Truth for us is not a system of thought. Truth is not created. Truth is. Christ is the Truth. Truth is a person. Truth is not limited within our apprehension of it. Truth transcends us; we can never come to the full comprehension of Truth. The search for Truth is a search for the person of Christ. Truth is the Mystery of the person of Christ; and, because it is a person, the Mystery is inseparably linked with the event: the event of the encounter. Mystery and event are one. The Mystery, for the Orthodox mind, is a precise and austere reality. It is Christ, and it is to meet Christ."

- *"If you miss the understanding of the Incarnation, the in-fleshing, the making visible of the invisible, you'll misunderstand the reason why the Orthodox Church uses so many visible things to worship and to pray."*

Many times our Lord used created things like spittle and dirt, the hem of a garment, water, bread, and wine, to manifest the power of God to us. As the learned Dr. Thomas Howard said, at a conference in Oklahoma City, "The Gospel is heavy with matter." (RTB pg 39).

- *"The King of the universe, because He loves His creation, becomes part of His creation to undo all of the knots of the fall so that nothing stands in your way of achieving what you were made to be in the first place—God's intimate companion—and enjoying all of the rights and privileges of a person created in the image of God, to be made in His likeness."*

Questions for discussion

As you consider this idea of "making visible the invisible" what comes to mind?

_____

_____

_____

_____

When we say we seek to "undo all the knots of the fall" what does this image bring up?

_____

_____

_____

In your opinion, is this kind of restoration a worthy or even achievable goal for a religion? Why or why not?

_____

_____

_____

_____

Session 12: *Our Ultimate Purpose*

"But the Helper, the Holy Spirit, whom the Father will send in My name, He will teach you all things, and bring to your remembrance all things that I said to you." —JOHN 14:26

"As the Lord put on the body, leaving behind all principality and power, so Christians put on the Holy Spirit, and are at rest." —ST. MACARIUS THE GREAT, *Spiritual Homilies*

Overview

The Holy Spirit leads the Church into all truth. We are constantly growing and changing in a culture that values growth and change. We live in a culture of the "now." Growth and change are not bad things so long as the growth and change are tempered with guidance and wisdom. The role of the person of the Holy Spirit in the Orthodox tradition is that of the "Helper" (or "Counselor" in some translations of the verse from the book of John). Having access to this helper or counselor as we move through our lives connects us to the person of God, the Father, and to the person of Jesus Christ. The Creator of all things and all people is the best source of guidance, the best source of wisdom.

In the wider community of the Orthodox Church, the Body of Christ, this same force—this wonderful counselor—guides us. This is the very ministry of the Holy Spirit as it pertains to the Church at large as well as the life of its members. The reason the Orthodox Church is called the "Church of the Holy Spirit" is because she has such a powerful understanding of the work of the Holy Spirit in the history of the Body of Christ.

The Church, then, is a perpetual Pentecost because the actual communion of the Church means that we follow the lives of those before us. They were led by the same Spirit that now leads us. The Holy Spirit, being God and eternal, protects the Church from the whims of fickle human cultures that change and shift.

KEY POINTS:

- *"God tells us this about Himself, and this is significant. From the Father, the Son is eternally begotten. From the Father, the Holy Spirit eternally proceeds, coequal, coeternal, the one God as Father, Son, and Holy Spirit. The scripture even declares that the Holy Spirit proceeds from the Father."*

In the Godhead, we have the Heavenly Father, called by the Scripture the one God. We also have from Him, by eternal generation or birth, the Son. And from this same Father, we have, by eternal procession, another divine person who is the Holy Spirit, a divine person who is as divine as the Father and the Son. This can be seen best in John 15:26: "When the Counselor comes, whom I will send to you from the Father, the Spirit of truth, who proceeds from the Father, He will testify about Me." The Holy Spirit teaches us about Christ and helps to form the character of Christ in us. He is the Lord of the Church and makes us into the Body of Christ.

- *"The Holy Spirit constitutes the Body of Christ in the earth so that what was localized in one God-man in Palestine so many centuries ago now gets spread over the whole earth. The Holy Spirit comes. The Comforter is coming to do the work that Jesus Christ did throughout the whole earth."*

This is the Holy Trinity that Orthodoxy seeks to know and worship. In fact, this view of the Holy Trinity permeates every aspect of Orthodox worship; prayers repeated three times; the sign of the cross made by a believer every time the Holy Trinity is mentioned; and even specific hymns like the Trisagion, or Thrice-Holy Hymn: Holy God, (the Father), Holy Mighty (the Son), Holy Immortal One (the Holy Spirit).

- *"That crucible of learning how to be in communion is what the work of the Holy Spirit is meant to foster and grow in our hearts right now, so where the Holy Spirit leads the Church, all of those places where He leads us is meant to help us build communion and intimacy with God and with each other."*

- *"The present work of the Holy Spirit is to reconstitute the incarnated son of God in every place in the world, and so the person of the Holy Spirit constitutes the Church, the Body of Christ, and makes the Body of Christ present."*

This kind of unity, of loving communion, of full relationship, will revolutionize your relationship with your spouse, your children, with everyone. Seeing each person created in His image and seeing ourselves as being grafted into the Church, the Body of Christ, we can now begin to grasp what is meant by our celebration of communion together and the ultimate goal of our salvation as reconciliation with ourselves, each other and, finally, God Himself.

Questions for discussion

Having come this far in the series, how would you describe the relationship between the three "persons" of God?

_____

_____

_____

_____

What images do the terms "Comforter" and "Wonderful Counselor" bring to mind for you?

_____

_____

_____

_____

What sources of guidance and wisdom do you look toward as you move through times of big change or growth?

_____

_____

_____

_____

Session 13: *Salvation as Participation*

"But above all these things put on love, which is the bond of perfection. And let the peace of God rule in your hearts, to which also you were called in one body; and be thankful. Let the word of Christ dwell in you richly in all wisdom, teaching and admonishing one another in psalms and hymns and spiritual songs, singing with grace in your hearts to the Lord."
—Colossians 3:14–16

"O wonder of wonders that Christ's spirit is united to our spirit, His will is one with ours, His flesh becomes our flesh, His blood flows in our veins. What spirit is ours when it is possessed by His, our will when led captive by His, our clay when set on fire by His flame."
—St. Nicholas Cabasilas

Overview

At the heart of the Orthodox practice, we find the Divine Liturgy. Within this weekly worship is the Eucharist, the communion of the people. Many Christian traditions participate in "communion" in one way or another. In the Orthodox tradition, the practice takes place every week and in the same form that has been followed for centuries.

The word *Eucharist* comes from the Greek word εὐχαριστία. Like many other words in Orthodoxy, we transliterate rather than translate. The word means, literally, thanksgiving or gratitude. We call the elements of the Eucharist the "gifts." These gifts are given to God so that He may fill them with Himself and that we might then receive Him in the Eucharist, or as we call it the *Holy Mystery*.

This mystery of the Eucharist is vital to the Orthodox life. The use of the physical to worship God constitutes a restoration of the high calling of humanity as the caretakers of the physical world. We use all of our senses in the worship, the entirety of the physical experience—sight, sound, touch, taste, and smell. These gifts are not only for ourselves, but as we are reminded every week in the Liturgy, *"We offer You these gifts from Your own gifts, in all and for all."*

We believe that the elements we present, the bread and the wine, become the very body and blood of Christ. The Orthodox do not purport to be able to explain or understand how this happens, but we believe that it does happen, and that this Holy Mystery helps to restore us, body and soul.

KEY POINTS:

- *"The reason why we're very physical in our worship is because we genuinely value and believe in the Incarnation. The invisible has become visible and we also believe that creation is very good."*

Somehow along the way, someone got the idea that creation was bad or evil. This idea was that there were two worlds, an upper world of heavenly or spiritual things (good things), and a "lower" world of matter (bad things). Only the spiritual world is important, and thus the "natural" or lower world is unimportant. Not so! In fact, in the very first part of Genesis we read that God Himself said that creation is good; in fact, everything God created is very good (Gen. 1:31).

- *"The Holy Spirit gathers us from all corners of the area of our community, we gather in one place and we constitute the body of Christ—and what do we do? We take our work and we offer it to God and we say, 'God, we offer You these gifts from Your own gifts on behalf of all and for all.'"*

Salvation, rather than being simply a rescuing from hell and judgment, is reconciliation between the Father and us. Salvation is a reversal of the effects of the fall. What once was lost is now restored in Christ. The Divine Mysteries of the Church reflect and manifest this to us and to the world. They allow the salvation purchased for us by Christ to be seen in this dark world.

- *"When the Orthodox Church talks about healing, it doesn't just talk about making our headache go away. It means healing us at the deepest place of our illness, which is always in our soul."*

Throughout Orthodox worship, and in everyday Orthodox prayers, the physical aspects of our devotion are plain to see. We have discussed the Orthodox understanding of the Divine Mysteries and attitude concerning the physical world. We have said that God likes matter and He has every intention of redeeming His creation. In the Orthodox view of the mysteries, we get to manifest that ultimate victory of God over the enemies of His creation now, in the Church, by using physical creation to glorify God and tell the Good News.

- *"We stand in awe of the goodness and the mercy of our God to put into place everything that will heal the brokenness of my own personal soul and give me the grace to be in communion."*

The Orthodox Church has always maintained that all of creation, from angel to ant, from water to iron, is God's good creation and was meant to reflect and participate in God's glory. It is part of God's plan of redemption to restore that goodness to creation through Christ and He has made a start in His new community of faith, the Church.

Questions for discussion

What has been your previous experience with the practice of "communion"?

_____

_____

_____

_____

When faced with the concept of "mystery" in this way, what occurs to you?

_____

_____

_____

_____

The physicality of the Orthodox Church is evident it its worship. What kinds of physical practices do you employ in your daily life? What gifts do you find in those practices?

_____

_____

_____

_____

Session 14: *Orthodox Worship*

"But if all prophesy, and an unbeliever or an uninformed person comes in, he is convinced by all, he is convicted by all. And thus the secrets of his heart are revealed; and so, falling down on his face, he will worship God and report that God is truly among you."
—1 CORINTHIANS 14:24–25

"When you look at the candles and lamps burning in Church, rise in thought from the material fire to the immaterial fire of the Holy Ghost, 'for our God is a consuming fire.' When you see and smell the fragrant incense, rise in thought to the spiritual fragrance of the Holy Ghost, 'for we are unto God a sweet savor of Christ.' "—ST. JOHN OF KRONSTADT, *My Life in Christ*

Overview

The Orthodox worship, the Divine Liturgy in particular, can be a foreign experience for the casual observer. The Liturgy meets us at every sensory level, engaging the whole person. The worship is active, the members are participants, and the audience is Christ alone.

Visually, we are engaged by the architecture of the space, the presence of murals on the walls, icons greeting us throughout the space, the royal doors that lead to the altar—the Holy of Holies. The priests' vestments, sometimes ornate, sometimes more plain, change according to the Church calendar as well as the place at which we find ourselves in the Liturgy itself. There is much to see in the Orthodox worship and we are called to "be attentive."

This call for attentiveness is heard throughout the services, a reminder to listen well and be present. Scripture and song are chanted and sung. The human voice is lifted to glorify God. Sound, like imagery, plays a significant part in the Liturgy. We smell the incense and candles.

We taste the bread and wine, the body and blood of Christ. We touch with prostrations, the sign of the cross, the greeting of one's neighbors, veneration of the icons, and it is all for the glory and worship of God. It is the Liturgy, the work of His people.

KEY POINTS:

- *"We are meant to be in God's presence and be in communion with God, and so the Orthodox worship is about the Body of Christ constituting herself and gathering together to offer our adoration and worship to God."*

To see what Orthodoxy believes, you must experience Orthodox worship. The Orthodox believe that their worship reflects what they believe. This is based on an old Latin phrase—*lex orandi, lex credendi est*—"The rule of prayer is the rule of faith."

- *"The Orthodox Church is interested in being timeless because, precious friends, I'm going to be in eternity a whole lot longer than I'm going to be on this earth, and so I need something in my life that reorients my life towards eternal things, and not just the temporary."*

All in all, the underlying consistency of the worship of God by the people of God is preserved, and this is as it should be. God first began to teach humanity how to properly honor Him, not for God's benefit, but for ours. It is this worship centered on awe and beauty that teaches prideful mankind to realize the overwhelming glory of our loving and awesome God, who, as we hear in our hymns at Divine Liturgy, is the "only lover of mankind."

- *"When you enter the church you enter the western door moving towards the east to remind you that you're moving from darkness to light, from chaos to order, from confusion to peace."*

Orthodox worship, maintaining the continuity of worship through the ages, embraces my whole person. Each time we gather to worship God, I am reminded in countless subtle and not so subtle ways that God is interested in redeeming my whole life, not just my mind.

- *"Every way a human can receive information, we're maximalistic in the Orthodox Church, so we use every avenue possible to communicate the focus of communion in our Orthodox worship."*

Orthodox worship engages me on every level of my human experience and, whether I realize it or not, this worship is changing me and teaching me the Faith. This idea of "maximalistic" worship then changes us when we come together, from an audience to a congregation. This rich heritage of worship in the Orthodox Church is the birthright of all believers in Christ. It is the regular, worthy offering of our adoration to our Savior and God.

Questions for discussion

It is said that most people fall into one category of learning or another—auditory, visual, or tactile. Which feels closest to your way of learning and understanding?

_____

_____

_____

_____

When you think of "worship" what comes to mind first?

_____

_____

_____

_____

Does this Orthodox notion of Liturgy challenge your personal understanding of worship? How?

_____

_____

_____

_____

Session 15: *A Beautiful Rhythm*

"As each one has received a gift, minister it to one another, as good stewards of the manifold grace of God. If anyone speaks, let him speak as the oracles of God. If anyone ministers, let him do it as with the ability which God supplies, that in all things God may be glorified through Jesus Christ, to whom belong the glory and the dominion forever and ever. Amen."
—1 Peter 4:10–11

"When the soul knows the love of God by the Holy Spirit, then he clearly feels that the Lord is our own Father, the closest, dearest Father, the best. And there is not greater happiness than to love God with all the mind and heart, and our neighbor as our self. And when this love is in the soul, then all things bring joy to the soul." —St. Silouan the Athonite

Overview

The practice of Orthodoxy affects every aspect of the life of an Orthodox Christian. Our sense of time is oriented around the Church calendar. That calendar is centered on the Feast of Feasts—Pascha (Orthodox Easter). Throughout the year, we celebrate daily the lives of the saints, the history of the Church, the consistent nature of a prayer life, and the nurturing and enrichment of our "time." We fill our time with the practice in order to be formed by it.

Our sense of space, too, is formed by this practice, a daily working out of our faith. We set up places of prayer in our houses called "Prayer Corners," filled with icons, incense, and prayer books. We orient our living spaces to reflect the nature of our faith, and the practices we embrace.

Through these consistent and ancient practices of prayer, fasting, and an adherence to the Church calendar, we are "Christianizing" our time and space, changing our perception of the world and re-orienting ourselves to be in the best possible relationship to God, to our friends and family, to the world, and to ourselves. The life of Christ becomes the measure of our day, week, month, and year. And the space of our lives is thus filled with remembrances of the Kingdom.

KEY POINTS:

- *"We're being made to be in communion, not division and separation, so there's continuity. This continuity is consistent, the Holy Spirit. Ever since God said, 'Let there be light,' the darkness has not overcome it. The light has continued to grow, and that's growing further still in the Church of our Lord Jesus Christ. Our time is now reoriented to the life of Jesus Christ."*

We understand ourselves, our world, and our relationships, in terms of Christ's life and gift. We see all the world, all people, events, and places through our union with Christ, therefore in the light of His love and grace.

- *"Heaven is being with people you've learned how to love."*

All these things are there to teach us how to enjoy living forever in communion. We become transformed through these activities as our body, soul, and Spirit all participate in the indwelling formative power of the Most Holy Spirit.

- *"When I learn to pray with the discipline of the Church through the Jesus Prayer, 'Lord Jesus Christ, Son of God, have mercy upon me, the sinner,' every moment can be changed. My hours, my days, my weeks, my months, my seasons, all Christianized by the presence of God."*

We seek to make our time an expression of *orthodoxa* (right worship) and *orthopraxis* (right conduct). The way we do this is through the celebration of our life in the Blessed Holy Trinity, the celebration of the life of Christ and the events of His saints throughout history as well as in our present age.

- *"Time is where we exist, but also our space is Christianized. I make one place holy so that I can learn how to make all places holy. Even my space is Christianized by me setting apart a space on the earth to build the temple of God."*

The Holy Table/the Cross of Christ/the Body of Christ is realized as the center of the real world. He is the "Axis of the World"; everything that *is* revolves around Him, and comes forth from Him. He is the Source of Life. The entire cosmos finds its orientation and center there, in Him. We find our "Center" in Christ's own life.

Questions for discussion

The idea of "communion" or "community" has been woven through this series. How do you see "community" as it pertains to your faith life?

_____

_____

_____

_____

Religious "practices" sometimes fall by the wayside in the absence of the historical Church. Do you adhere to any kind of "practice" either on your own or in your community of faith?

_____

_____

_____

_____

The concept of "eternity" in the life of the Orthodox Christian is profound. That we believe death has been defeated is a foundational element. What impact does this idea of having "eternal life" have on the way you live now?

_____

_____

_____

_____

Session 16: *The Journey Continues*

"For this reason we also, since the day we heard it, do not cease to pray for you, and to ask that you may be filled with the knowledge of His will in all wisdom and spiritual understanding; that you may walk worthy of the Lord, fully pleasing Him, being fruitful in every good work and increasing in the knowledge of God; strengthened with all might, according to His glorious power, for all patience and longsuffering with joy; giving thanks to the Father who has qualified us to be partakers of the inheritance of the saints in the light."
—COLOSSIANS 1:9–12

"The first stage of this tranquility consists in silencing the lips when the heart is excited. The second, in silencing the mind when the soul is still excited. The goal is a perfect peacefulness even in the middle of the raging storm." —ST. JOHN CLIMACUS

Overview

This introduction to Orthodox Christianity is meant to give an overview of the faith. That there are a myriad of resources to learn about Orthodoxy is significant. Whether books, videos, or web pages, there is no shortage of "information."

The true next step requires more than the intellectual pursuit of Orthodoxy. It requires engagement and questioning, relationship building and participation, prayer and practice. Each of these things is meant to establish a pathway forward into the rich fullness of the tradition.

This moving river of the Orthodox Church can seem daunting and perhaps even dangerous. In order to move further into the faith and understand it from the inside, only relationship will suffice—with a spiritual Father, local priest, and community of faith, but also by familiarizing yourself with the practices of prayer and Liturgy. Taking the next step, moving beyond the beginning set forth here, is courageous and not to be taken lightly.

KEY POINTS:

- *"You can't become Orthodox by watching a video series. You can't become Orthodox by reading a book. If you want to know how to be Orthodox, you have to learn to pray. You have to learn to worship."*

We have a thirst for true being, a thirst for reality, and God is the Source of this true being, the source of this reality. Only God can quench our thirst. Christ came to give us the Holy Spirit and fill us with Living Water (Jn. 7:37–39).

- *"You can only be catechized in communion. Remember what we said about the Church? The Church understands herself as communal. We're a family. You can only be a family, in a family. We're a family."*

When Christians from different denominations meet, they usually get around to asking, "What do you believe?" It's a way of comparing notes and discovering whether one has common beliefs with others, and of saying, "Who are you?" For Westerners, it is also a way to discover whether that person is in error. But for Orthodox, a relationship must first ensue. It is not simply a person's beliefs that must be discovered, it is the person himself. That cannot be done except on a long-term relationship basis. We must first give ourselves to one another unreservedly; similar to what happened with the apostles in the book of Acts (2:42-47).

- *"The Church will give you everything you need to be ready to step into this moving river of the Orthodox faith, without being swept away. She will give you every tool you need, so that when you step into this river, you won't lose your footing."*

We have a responsibility to those of bygone days to deliver this faith to those who come after us. That requires some hard work on our part. The Church is not the end of our journey, but the beginning of it.

- *"The whole point of this rhythm of life is to have you come to what the Fathers called* nepsis. *A sober joy, life doesn't take you too high, life doesn't take you too low. That no matter what the outside circumstances, your life is at an even keel."*

This "sober joy" we find in *nepsis*, which is literally, "wakefulness," is about the transfiguration of our experience of "ordinary reality" by the grace and presence of the Most Holy Spirit. We are awake, attentive, and alive to Christ. It is what happens to human consciousness when transformed by the indwelling experience of the Holy Spirit and therefore the experience of communion with the Blessed and Life-giving Trinity.

Questions for discussion

Considering the "sober joy" of *nepsis*, this wakefulness, how do you find your even keel in life?

_____

_____

_____

_____

Thinking through the whole of the sessions, what is the one idea, concept, or quote that was most striking or profound to you?

_____

_____

_____

_____

If you had a reservation about visiting and experiencing an Orthodox Liturgy, what would it be?

_____

_____

_____

_____

"MOST ASSUREDLY, I SAY TO YOU, UNLESS ONE IS BORN OF WATER AND THE SPIRIT, HE CANNOT ENTER THE KINGDOM OF GOD."

JOHN 4:1–14

Ambo - In the ancient Church, a raised platform in the nave, near the middle of the building between the solea and the Royal Doors, used for Scripture readings and where the homily was sometimes given. Usually, the celebrant gave the homily from the Soleas and the bishop gave the homily from his chair, which in ancient times may have been behind the altar, or to the side of the iconostasis. The ambo was used for teaching and presenting newly baptized, and for the "Ambo Prayer"—that prayer which is prayed by the presider at the end of the Liturgy. Contemporary practice in America, probably due to Western influence, has been to place the ambo on the northern side of the Solea, opposite the bishop's throne. In ancient times it was in the Nave, so that the Gospel would be read where Christ dwells—in "the midst of his people."

Anamnesis - ("remembrance"); The liturgical prayer that begins, "Mindful, therefore, of this command of the Savior, and all that was done for us: the cross, the tomb, the resurrection on the third day. . ."

Anaphora - The offering of the liturgical gifts for consecration, beginning with the words, "Let us stand with dignity! Let us stand in awe, and in the peace of Christ, let us with gratitude lift up our hearts. . ." It continues with the invocation (*epiclesis*) of the Holy Spirit: "Asking, praying, and beseeching you to send down your Holy Spirit upon us and upon these gifts. . ." It includes the consecration of the gifts, the thanksgiving prayers, the Lord's Prayer, and finally, the offering of the elements to the faithful.

Antimension - a consecrated cloth decorated with icons, sewn with holy relics, and bearing the signature of the bishop. It means "in place of the table," and refers to a time when there was no consecrated Holy Table for the Eucharistic celebration, and the antimension served instead of a Holy Table. It dates from the 8th century, and today has come to represent the permission of the bishop for a priest to celebrate the Eucharistic rite.

Antiphon - Verses or refrains sung alternately by two choirs, cantors, or by the people. Sometimes it may be used as a refrain sung between verses of Psalms.

Apocrypha - Hidden books included in the Septuagint and Vulgate but excluded from the Jewish and Protestant canons of the Old Testament. See "Deutero-Canonical" writings.

Apollinarius - (A.D. 310–390) An upholder of Orthodoxy against the Arians, became bishop of Laodicea in 361. When the Council of Alexandria (362), chaired by Athanasius, attributed a human soul to Christ, his teachings were brought forth for criticism. He separated from the Orthodox Church in 375. In 377, a council in Rome, chaired by Pope Damasus, also condemned Apollinarius. At the Second Ecumenical Council in Constantinople (381), his teaching was again condemned. Convinced that only the unchangeable Divine Logos could be the Savior of man, Apollinarius denied the presence of a human mind or soul in Christ. This enabled him to stress the unity of the Godhead and the humanity in the person of Christ, but denied the completeness of Christ's humanity.

Apology, apologetics - "To defend," or "to give an answer" for one's beliefs. Apologetics is a discipline of theology that attempts to defend or vindicate Christian beliefs. An "apologist" is one who writes a treatise to defend or explain some aspect of the faith.

Apophatic - *Apophasis* is Greek for Anegation and an apophatic theology is a Anegative theology. The counterpart of apophasis is kataphasis, "affirmation;" hence the terms "apophatic" and "cataphatic." To explain the mystical meaning of the doctrine of angels, the title of the 3rd chapter of *The Mystical Theology* by Pseudo-Dionysius the Areopagite asks: "Which are the cataphatic theologies, and which are the apophatic?" He replies that the central doctrines of the catholic faith, such as the Trinity and the incarnation, are affirmations. But, when speaking about the transcendent, ". . . my argument now rises from what is below up to the transcendent, and the more it climbs, the more language falters, and when it has passed up and beyond ascent, it will turn silent completely, since it will finally be at one with him who is indescribable. In another treatise (Corpus Areopagiticum) he says, "The Deity is far beyond every manifestation of being and life." According to Jaroslav Pelikan, in *The Melody of Theology,* that is why ". . . the Bible resorted to such negative terms as invisible, as in the oxymoron of the locus classicus for natural theology (Rom. 1:20) His invisible attributes, that is to say his everlasting power and deity, have been visible . . ."

Evagrius of Pontus said, "A God cannot be grasped by the mind. If he could be grasped, he would not be God." Kallistos Ware, in *The Orthodox Way,* writes: ". . . yet symbols alone are insufficient to convey the transcendence and otherness of God. To point at the *mysterium tremendum*, we need to use negative as well as affirmative statements, saying what God is not rather than what He is. Without this use of the way of negation, of what is termed the apophatic approach, our talk about God becomes gravely misleading" (p. 16).

Asceticism - (Gk. askesis); A system of personal discipline for the purpose of developing virtues. When Christ called His disciples, He said, "If anyone would come after me, he must deny himself and take up his cross and follow me. "(Mt. 16:24) The two sides of asceticism are self-denial and following Christ.

Bishop - (Gk. episcopos); The English term bishop is an Anglo-Saxon derivative of the term "episcopos," a transliteration of the Greek term. A bishop is one of the ranks of clergy, deacon and presbyter (or "priest") being the other two ranks. Proto-presbyter, Archdeacon, Archbishop, and Archimandrite are simply administrative titles relating to the functions of a diocese or monastic community. Only the offices of deacon, priest, and bishop are considered ordinations by the "laying on of hands" and the invocation of the Holy Spirit on the candidate. At first, the terms "episcopos" and "presbyter" were used interchangeably: "From Miletus, Paul sent to Ephesus for the elders (presbyteros) of the Church. When they arrived, he said to them . . . Guard yourselves and all the flock of which the Holy Spirit has made you overseers (episcopos)." (Acts 20:17,28). Early in the 2nd century, the three ranks of clergy became clearly distinct, with the bishop as the head of the Church and presbyters (priests) his assistants. While deacons and priests may be ordained by their bishop, a bishop must be ordained by two or three other bishops.

Catechesis - Instruction given to candidates (catechumens) for Christian baptism, or for those wanting to become members of a local Church who have already been baptized.

Catechism - A manual of Christian doctrine. Originally applied to the oral instruction on the faith given to children and adults preparing for baptism. The name has come to signify the book used for teaching, and the entire series of teachings given to catechumens.

Catechumen - One undergoing instruction and training before being baptized. It has come to include those who have been baptized in another communion who wish to become members of the Orthodox Church. In ancient times, catechumens had to stand in a particular place and were dismissed before the Anaphora. In the Roman Catholic communion, catechumens usually leave after the Liturgy of the Word and go to a class of instruction. In Orthodox Churches, they normally remain through the Liturgy of the Table, but do not partake of the Eucharist. Catechumens are received into Eucharistic fellowship either by baptism or by "normalization" of one's baptism.

Cherubic Hymn - The hymn sung as an introduction to the second part of the liturgy (the "Liturgy of the Table," or the "Liturgy of the Faithful"). It is sung as the elements are being carried from the Table of Preparation to the Altar. This procession is called the Great Entrance.

Cherubim - The second-highest order of the nine orders of angels. The cherubim attend God and are close to Him, entering into the very glory of His presence. While some theologians say that they "protect" God from any blasphemy or unholy acts, St. John Chrysostom implies that God needs no such protection. Rather, they are the only beings (other than human beings who have been "deified") who may come close enough to view the "glory" of God without being destroyed. Even so, they cover their eyes and constantly cry out to one another, "Holy, holy, holy!" St. John Chrysostom writes: "For what reason, pray tell, did they extend their wings and cover their faces? For

what reason could it be, except that they could not bear the lightning and the flashes of radiance leaping from the throne? Anyone who is not himself light unalloyed does not see the pure essence itself. . ."

Christian Year - (Church Year, or Liturgical Year); A portrayal and remembrance of the events of the life of Christ in a cycle of prayers and rites throughout the year, beginning on September 1st. There are 12 major feasts, 8 minor ones, 4 fasting periods and the cycle of saints' days (each day of the year commemorating the death—the passing into "life," thus the "birth" day—of one or more saints).

Chrism - (the Mystery or Rite of Chrism, or Chrismation); Anointing as an act of setting apart to the glory of Jesus Christ, the "anointed one." St. Cyril of Jerusalem called it the "mystic chrism," and in the canons of the Synod of Laodicea (A.D. 360), it is called the "holy chrism." Chrism (Chrismation) signifies the "sealing" of the gift of the Holy Spirit on the believer, as well as conveying the "fullness" of God's presence in the Holy Spirit, as well as the graces and gifts of the Spirit. It is a personal Pentecost, a re-enactment of the day of Pentecost when the disciples were gathered in an upper room and the Holy Spirit fell on them (see Acts 2). The word is also used to refer to the oil used in Chrism—olive oil usually mixed with perfumes or spices and blessed in a specific ceremony. Only bishops may consecrate the chrism (or Holy Myron). Holy Chrism may also be used in consecrating altars, for anointing priests, and at other ceremonies.

Communion - see Eucharist.

Confession - One of the mysteries (or sacraments) of the Orthodox Church. It is also called the "Mystery of Metanoia (repentance)." Confession focuses on the inner change in the believer, rather than the act of confessing one's errors to a priest. In the ancient Church, confession of sin was done publicly (see Ac. 19:18). Later, this practice was given up (in the 3rd century), during the Decian persecution, as many Christians had denied their faith in the fear of persecution.

Cloud of Unknowing, the - Probably the greatest Western book on mystical theology, written by an unknown monk in the 14th century. Originally written in Middle English, the author explains how all thoughts and concepts must be buried beneath a "cloud of forgetting," while our love must rise toward God hidden in the "cloud of unknowing."

Creed - From the Latin *credo*, to believe. The first word of the Nicene and Apostle's Creeds. The Orthodox refer to the Nicene Creed as "the Creed," since it is the only creed approved by an Ecumenical Council. Only the Nicene Creed is recognized as authoritative by the Orthodox Church. The practice of reciting this creed during the liturgy began sometime in the 5th century.

Deacon - (Gr. diakonos); One of the ranks of clergy. Originally, the first seven deacons (Ac. 6:1–7) were elected and ordained for serving the poor and distributing alms. Because of the deacon's duties, the office held great power. Eventually, the archdeacon became the chief administrative officer of the bishop. The first Ecumenical Council limited the powers of deacons. Ceremonial duties of deacons involve assisting in the liturgy. Practically, the diaconate has been used for centuries as a time of training and a stepping-stone to the priesthood, although its original purpose was to ordain those to service who were to serve as deacons for life.

Deaconess - Women in the early Church who performed certain functions were called deaconesses. "I commend to you our sister, Phoebe, a servant (diakonon) of the church in Cenchrea." (Ro. 16:1) The deaconesses were to help care for the poor and the sick, to be present at interviews of women by bishops, priests, or deacons, to introduce women catechumens, to conduct the baptism of women, and to administer the Eucharist to those women who were sick and unable to attend the Eucharistic gathering of the Church.

Deutero-Canonical writings - Those writings of the Old Testament contained in the Septuagint and Vulgate, but not in the Jewish and Protestant canons of the Old Testament.

Doxology - A liturgical prayer in which praise and glory are ascribed to the Trinity. The "minor" doxology is a prayer that begins, "Glory be to the Father, and to the Son, and to the Holy Spirit." The "major" doxology begins with the angelic hymn found in Luke (2:14), "Glory to God in the highest, and on earth peace among men with whom he is pleased." (NASB)

Economia - A timely and logically defensible deviation from a canonically-established rule for the sake of bringing salvation or to provide for a justifiable change in practice. This deviation does not allow for the violation of dogmatic boundaries of the rule that is being changed or set aside. The Church, in her constituted authority, being the steward of the graces of the Holy Spirit, may decide that the strict observance of a rule would not (in a certain case) contribute to or be amenable to the preservation of unity and order within the body. In some cases, the particular rule simply cannot be observed to the letter as tradition or canon law has established it. For example, in the case of an infant facing imminent death, any Orthodox layperson, or even a non-Orthodox believer, may baptize the infant by effusion (pouring of water) in the name of the Trinity. If no water is available, the baptism may be done without water by holding the child in the air and making the sign of the cross with the infant in the name of the Trinity. Thus, a rule is not abolished, but simply set aside or bypassed for a time through this principle. The cases should be times when an unusual circumstance requires a timely and temporary use of this measure.

Ecumenical Councils - Orthodoxy recognizes seven General Councils of the Church, and the decisions of these councils have been accepted by both East and West as authoritative. These councils are (1) Nicea, A.D. 325; (2) Constantinople, A.D. 381; (3) Ephesus, A.D. 431; (4) Chalcedon, A.D. 451; (5) II Constantinople, A.D. 553; (6) III Constantinople, A.D. 681; (7) II Nicea, A.D. 787.

Eucharist - From the Greek, *eucharistos*, "to give thanks." It is usually applied to the communion that commemorates both the prayer of thanksgiving of Christ as the last supper and the giving to the faithful of the elements, the body and blood of Christ. Partaking of the elements is called "sharing in the Eucharist." To be Eucharistic means to be one who participates in partaking of the elements.

Exapostalarion - Originally a hymn invoking the divine light, today these hymns frequently refer to the celebration of the day, and may or may not refer to the divine light. Those used for Lent are called *photogogika*, and these refer to the divine light.

Fall - The act of disobedience by which mankind lost primal innocence and acquired the possibility of sinning and pain. The Fall resulted in a breaking of communion with God, which resulted in death.

Fathers - see patristic.

Fish - In both Christian art and literature, the fish is a symbol of Christ. It was used as early as the 2nd century. Tertullian speaks of the believers in baptism as "little fish," alluding to the second birth in the waters. The Greek name for fish is IXOYE, representing Jesus, Christ, God, Son, Savior, or, "Jesus Christ, Son of God, Savior." In the 4th and 5th centuries, the fish became an emblem for the Eucharist.

Grace - The uncreated energy of God by which He shares His divine life with us. Grace is a participation in the union and intermingling of Christ with the believer—the life of Christ. It is not by merit that we achieve this union, but through the love of God, which is offered to us without reservation and without cost.

Great Entrance - The part of the liturgy when the elements—the bread and wine—are carried by the deacon or priest in solemn procession from the table of preparation through the Holy Doors and to the Holy Table.

Holy Doors - The doors leading from the Soleas to the Altar area, through which the presider and others enter when celebrating the Service of the Table, through which the holy gifts are brought to the Holy Table at the Great Entrance, and through which the Gospels are brought back to the Holy Table at the end of the Liturgy.

Holy Table - The Eucharistic (consecrated) table in the

altar area, used for the consecration of the holy bread and wine. While some fathers use the terms altar and table synonymously, today the altar area usually signifies the sanctuary. Originally made of wood (3-feet tall and 3-feet square), the wooden tables in metropolitan areas began to be replaced by stone or marble, with a marble slab on top. All stone tables have relics of martyrs entombed in them, with inscriptions. In some places, the tables are made of gold and precious metals.

Icon - Depictions of persons or events, painted on wood (also in mosaic, with ivory, or other materials). They may represent Christ, Mary, or the saints who are venerated. They may also depict events described in the Scriptures, in the life of Christ, or in the lives of the saints. Icons are called "windows into heaven," since they help us focus on heavenly things. It is believed that any honor given to an icon passes on to the person appearing on the icon. While veneration is given to icons, worship is reserved for God alone.

Iconoclast, iconoclasm - A "fighter against icons," those who destroy or oppose the veneration of icons. The veneration of icons was upheld at the Seventh Ecumenical Council in Nicea, A.D. 787.

Iconostasis - A row of icons that separates the altar area (sometimes called the sanctuary) from the nave (the main part of the church). The iconostasis has an opening in the center, called the holy doors, since this is where the elements of the Eucharist are brought in procession to the altar, and the North and South doors, which are used by the deacons and by those entering or exiting the altar area for other than liturgical reasons. The term "royal doors," sometimes used in reference to the iconostasis actually refers to the doorway between the narthex and the nave through which the people enter.

Jesus Prayer - "Lord Jesus Christ, Son of God, have mercy on me a sinner." This prayer, believed to originate with (and be a modification of) the prayer of the blind man, Bartimaeus (Mk. 10:47), has become a premier prayer among the Orthodox. It was used in particular by the Hesychasts, who repeated this prayer in rhythm with the breathing of the person praying, while concentrating on Christ.

Kontakion - (or kondakion); A liturgical hymn sung in the services, including the liturgy. Originally, a Kontakion was a long didactic poem with a short introductory hymn and a longer composition. Today, only the hymn and a shortened portion of the second part is retained. In practice, the Kontakion has become much more thematic than the Troparion, spelling out the message of the celebration more specifically than the Troparion.

Ladder of Divine Ascent, the - The most widely used handbook of the ascetic life in the Orthodox Church. Written by St. John Climacus (Gr. for "ladder"), while archimandrite of the monastery at Mt Sinai, in the early part of the 7th century. St. John was born around the middle of the 6th century, became a monk and spent 40 years in solitude, becoming leader of the famous monastery on Mt Sinai. The Ladder was written to answer an urgent need for an explanation of the problems, needs, and requirements of the monastic life. John, who called himself a "second-rate architect," detailed 30 steps or rungs on the ladder of the spiritual life, of virtues to be acquired or of vices to be surrendered.

Litany - A series of short petitions and exhortations given by the deacon or priest, and to which the people respond, "Lord, have mercy," "Grant it, O Lord," or "To you, O Lord."

Little Entrance - The time during the Liturgy when the Gospels are carried in procession from the Holy Table to the Ambo, while the "Alleluia" is sung, in preparation for the Gospel reading. In ancient times, the Gospels were not kept in the church, but were hidden until they were brought out for the Gospel reading, and then taken back into safekeeping. Now, the Gospels are kept on the Holy Table until the Little Entrance. They are then left on the Ambo, for the faithful to venerate when coming forward to receive the Eucharist. Afterward, the deacon brings the Gospels back to the Holy Table after the folding of the antimension.

Liturgy - From the Greek, *leitourgia,* "work of the people." Chiefly, it denotes the words and order of the Eucharist. There are three main Orthodox liturgies: (1) St. John Chrysostom, which is used mainly throughout the year; (2) St. Basil, used at specific times during the year; and (3) St. James, used primarily at Christmas. These are usually referred to as the Divine Liturgy. A fourth liturgy, that of the Presanctified Gifts, is performed normally on Wednesdays and Fridays of Great Lent.

Metanoia - Greek, *meta*—change; *noia*—mind. Repentance. Not only the sorrow of contrition or regret, but the fundamental conversion and turning of one's whole life toward God. See repentance.

Monarchianism - Also called patripassionism, Sabellianism, and modalism. In the Christian East, in the early centuries after Christ, the tendency was toward tritheism, while in the West, the tendency was toward the unity of the Godhead. This heresy tended to be a relationship of the Father in which Jesus was a mere man endued with the Holy Spirit.

Monogenes - The first word of a hymn addressed to Christ, "O Only-Begotten Son." It has traditionally been ascribed to the Emperor Justinian I (reigned A.D. 527-565).

Monophysitism - The belief that Christ's nature remains altogether divine and not human after the union (Incarnation), and that His human nature was swallowed up like a drop of wine in the ocean. This belief was condemned at the Council of Chalcedon (A.D. 451).

Monoenergism - The belief that only one energy animated Christ, the divine Word. It was condemned, along with monothelitism, at the Sixth Ecumenical Council, in Constantinople, A.D. 681.

Monothelitism - The belief that only one will was present in Christ. The emperor Heraclius attempted to find a formula acceptable to both Monophysites and Chalcedonians, stating that while there were two natures in Christ, there was one mode of activity, one energy. one will, the divine will. This was condemned at the Sixth Ecumenical Council in Constantinople, A.D. 681.

Mystery - (Gk. mysterion); An interaction between God and us; God's ways of dealing with and revealing Himself to us. It does not mean something baffling—an insoluble dilemma or problem. Rather, it signifies something that is revealed for our understanding but which we can never fully or exhaustively understand because it leads into the depth or darkness of God. The number of mysteries is infinite.

Narthex - The vestibule or antechamber leading to the Nave, from which it is usually separated by columns or rails. Catechumens in ancient times were only allowed to enter to the Narthex. Even today the first portion of the baptismal liturgy begins in the Narthex.

Nave - The main part of a temple, from the Royal Doors leading from the Narthex to the Soleas, where the people gather and worship.

New Testament - Those canonical writings of the Scriptures written either by an apostle of Christ or by someone close to the apostles. The four Gospels detail the life of Christ. The Acts is a brief history of some of the apostles and the early Christians. The letters are instructions from apostles (Paul, Peter, James, John) to either Churches or to persons. The Apocalypse is an apocalyptic account of the ongoing battle between the forces of evil and the Church.

Old Testament – (preferably "First Testament"); Those canonical writings of the Scriptures which tell the histories of the lives of a certain people, and God's dealings with them. They are sometimes called the "Hebrew Scriptures" since they comprised the Bible of the Jews. They were quoted by Christ and by the apostles as foretelling the events in the life of Christ (Mt. 26:54; Lu. 24:44; Ac. 3:18; Ac. 13:33; 1 Pe. 2:6).

Pantocrator - (all ruler); An icon painted in the dome of most Byzantine churches. Christ is depicted with open arms and in a gesture of blessing.

Pascha - From the Greek for Passover. It is the Orthodox word for Easter.

Patristic - (of the fathers); In *The Year of Grace of the Lord,* the author discusses how one defines a "father of the Church." We can summarize by saying that a father of the Church was at first used of those bishops who were at the Council of Nicea. Later, the bishops of the other councils were added, then worthy priests and laymen who were ecclesiastical writers, faithful witnesses, and who had Orthodoxy of doctrine. Such men as Origen and Eusebius of Caesarea, while being both ancient writers and living saintly lives, do not have the approval of the Church for their doctrine. While there is no official list of the fathers, it is generally agreed that the patristic age ended with St. John of Damascus, who died around A.D. 749.

Penitence - Sorrow for sins or faults. Contrition, compunction, remorse or regret for one's misdeeds. Mental anguish for past wrongs.

Pentecost - (fifty); The feast commemorating the descent of the Holy Spirit on the disciples gathered in the upper room detailed in the Acts of the Apostles (2:1–43). It is one of the 12 major feasts of the Christian Year.

Pentecostarion - The liturgical book containing the prayers and hymns used during the season between Holy Pascha (Easter) and the Sunday of All Saints.

Philokalia - A collection of writings between the 4th and 15th centuries by spiritual leaders of the Orthodox tradition. First published in Greek in 1782, and later translated into Russian. Outside of the Holy Scriptures, the *Philokalia* has had more influence than any other book in the recent history of the Church. Some of the themes dealt with in the *Philokalia* are intellection (the intuitive and discriminating sense by which we experience the spiritual), faith, discernment, love, God, wisdom, the passions, contemplative stillness, and union with God.

Presbyter - (Elder); In the ancient church, the terms presbyter and episcopos were used interchangeably. From the 2nd century, episcopos (bishop) has been used to refer to those presiding over a council (or group) of presbyters. Presbyter has been reduced (as a slang term) for priest (prest). The presbyters were given authority by the bishop in teaching, administration, and all the functions of the bishop except for ordination and consecrating altars and holy oil.

Presbytera - The wife of a presbyter. It is used as a gesture of respect for the priest's wife. Also used as Matushka.

Prokeimenon - (*pro* - before; *keimenon* - text); It refers to the hymn or Psalm sung before the Apostolic reading (the second or New Testament reading).

Prosphora - The round loaf of bread used in the consecration of the Eucharist.

Repentance - (metanoia); A change of mind. Not only sorrow, contrition, or regret, but a fundamental conversion and turning of one's whole life toward God. In Orthodox belief, repentance is more a life-style than an event in one's life. It involves all the actions of one's life in turning one from a worldly mindset to becoming converted in our intellect and our will.

Royal Doors - The doors or entrance leading from the Narthex (vestibule) to the Nave, where the faithful gather for worship. In ancient times, catechumens were not allowed to enter through the Royal Doors, but had to stay in the Narthex and then had to leave at the end of the Service of the Word, when the deacon cried out, "The Doors! The Doors!" when the Royal Doors were closed and only the faithful were allowed to be present during the Service of the Table.

Sabellianism - see also Monarchianism. There are no extent writings of Sabellius, so his teachings must be reconstructed through the writings of Tertullian and Hippolytus. Sabellius took the teachings of the Monarchians further, dealing with the problem of how to accept the deity of Christ and maintain the unity of God. As in Monarchianism, the Sabellians wished to safeguard monotheism and the deity of Christ, but their result was to confuse the persons of Father, Son, and Holy Spirit, reducing them to temporary manifestations (or revelations) of the one God. As Father, God (the divine monad) revealed Himself as Creator and Lawgiver. As Son, God revealed Himself as Redeemer. As Spirit, God revealed Himself as giver of grace. These were three different modes revealing the same person.

Sacrament - see mystery.

Salvation - The progressive infusion of the life of God, through deification, into the believer. By the Incarnation (the birth, life, death, burial, resurrection, and ascension) of Christ and the mysteries, every believer participates in the gracious offering of the divine life. Theosis is the journey of becoming "by grace what God is by nature." By God's gracious gift of grace, we are saved from Satan, sin, and death.

Seraphim - Those angelic creatures having six wings that Isaiah saw hovering above the throne of God (Is. 6:1-3). The Fathers have held from early times that the seraphim are a rank of angels and counterparts to the cherubim. They came to be ranked highest in the 9 orders of angels, followed by the cherubim.

Soleas - That area, usually part of a raised platform, that is between the nave and the area of the altar. It is the area in front of the holy doors where the celebrant and the deacon stand for certain parts of the liturgy.

Symbol - That which expresses, communicates, reveals, manifests, and participates in the reality of that which it symbolizes without losing its own nature and presence. A symbol unites different realities, intensifying our awareness and hunger for the other. However real a symbol may be and however well it communicates to us that other reality, its purpose is not to quench our thirst for that reality, but to intensify it.

Synaxarion - A brief account of the life of a saint. Also, a book of the accounts of the lives of saints.

Synaxis - A gathering of people for the purpose of worship.

Theotokos - ("mother of God," lit., God-bearer); Applied to the Virgin Mary by the Church Fathers. It was used to defend and define the full deity of Christ, since He who was born of Mary was fully God, "true God of true God." Nestorius and others attacked this term, saying that "God could not be five minutes old." They preferred the term Christotokos for St. Mary. But the 3rd Ecumenical Council (Ephesus, A.D. 431) and the 4th Council (Chalcedon, A.D. 451) upheld the use of this term and it has held an undisputed place in the Church since then.

Tradition - (Holy Tradition); The revelation of God delivered to faithful people through the prophets and apostles. The truths of the faith delivered by Christ and

His apostles to the Church. These truths have been revealed in the Scriptures, in the Ecumenical Councils, in the writings of the Fathers, in the liturgical books of the Church, and in the common faith of the Church. Those ecclesiastical traditions (small "t") referring to worship, polity, and the life of the Church, while deserving respect and honor, should be distinguished from Holy Tradition (capital T), which has a greater authority and deserves greater honor. It is believed that Holy Tradition has been established by the Holy Spirit in the life of the Church.

Triodion - (three odes); The liturgical book that contains the hymns used beginning on the 5th Sunday before Great Lent and ending on Saturday of Holy Week. The name comes from the fact that during this season three odes (hymns) are sung in place of the usual nine sung during Matins (Orthros).

Trisagion - ("thrice-holy"); The hymn that begins, "Holy God, holy Mighty, holy Immortal One . . ." sung during the Divine Liturgy.

Troparion - Originally, a poetic composition intended as a refrain to the chanting of the Psalms. It was used in various ways in times past, usually during processions. Today, Troparion usually refers to the thematic hymn of the feast sung at the conclusion of Vespers and at Matins.

Typicon - A liturgical manual containing the instructions for the order of hymns for certain feast days. It also contains directions for the celebration of the daily cycle, as well as the weekly (Octoechos) cycle, the monthly (Menaion) cycle, and the order of the various services for Holy Lent (Triodion) and Pentecost (Pentecostarion). A book of instructions for services.

Veneration - (honor); The Scriptures tell us to honor our father and mother (Eph. 6:2). The presbyters who direct the affairs of the Church well are to be given double honor (1 Ti. 5:17). Paul told the Philippians to honor men like Epaphroditus, since he risked his life for the work of Christ (Ph. 2:29-30). We are also admonished to honor widows (1 Ti. 5:3), the emperor (1 Pe. 2:17), wives (1 Pe. 3:7) and each other (Ro. 12:10). The Greek word translated "honor" is *time* (J4:Z). It means to place a value on some-one, a distinction, or reverential respect. In the King James translation of the Bible, the Greek word *doxa* ("glory") is sometimes translated "honor" (Jn. 5:41; 2 Cor. 6:8). The word "venerate" comes from a Greek word, *proskynesis*, which means reverential respect and honor, whether given to God (Jn. 4:21) or to man (Mt. 18:26). The Greek word *latreia* refers to worship or "adoration" that is reserved for God alone. Often, Protestants will accuse Orthodox believers of worship or adoration, when in actuality they are equating ado-ration with veneration. These are not the same thing. For Orthodox, veneration is the ladder to adoration. By this, we mean that by learning how to properly vener-ate those who are created in the image of God and to pay them honor, we learn how to properly adore the Blessed Trinity. If we do not love our brother, whom we can see, John writes, we cannot love God whom we can't see.

The Orthodox Study Bible
Thomas Nelson Publishers, June 2008
http://www.thomasnelson.com/the-orthodox-study-bible

St John of Damascus, On the Divine Images
translated by David Anderson
Crestwood, NY: St. Vladimir's Seminary Press, 1980.
https://www.amazon.com/Divine-Images-Apologies-Against-Attack/dp/0913836621

Introducing the Orthodox Church: Its Faith and Life
by Anthony M Coniaris
Minneapolis: Light and Life Publishing Co., 1982.
https://www.amazon.com/Introducing-Orthodox-Church-Faith-Life/dp/0937032255/

Eastern Orthodoxy: A Way of Life
by Anthony M Coniaris
Minneapolis: Light and Life Pub. Co.
http://www.light-n-life.com/eastern-orthodoxy-a-way-of-life.html

The Living God: A Catechism
translated by Olga Dunlop
NY: St Vladimir's Seminary Press, 2 vols., 1989.
http://www.archangelsbooks.com/proddetail.asp?prod=SVSCATECH-01

Let Us Attend: A Journey Through the Divine Liturgy
by Father Lawrence Farley
Ancient Faith Publishing
http://store.ancientfaith.com/let-us-attend/

The History of the Christian Church Until the Great Schism of 1054
by Thomas Herman
AuthorHouse, November 23, 2004
http://www.amazon.com/History-Christian-Church-Until-Schism/dp/141847326X/

The Mountain of Silence: A Search for Orthodox Spirituality
by Kyriacos C. Markides
Image; Reprint edition (November 19, 2002)
http://www.amazon.com/Mountain-Silence-Search-Orthodox-Spirituality/dp/0385500920/

Introducing Eastern Orthodox Theology
by Andrew Louth
IVP Academic, November 11, 2013
https://www.amazon.com/Introducing-Eastern-Orthodox-Theology-Andrew-ebook/dp/B00HUCPUTM/

Welcome to the Orthodox Church: An Introduction to Eastern Christianity
by Frederica Mathewes-Green
Paraclete Press, April 1, 2015
http://www.amazon.com/Welcome-Orthodox-Church-Introduction-Christianity/dp/1557259216/

Facing East: A Pilgrim's Journey into the Mysteries of Orthodoxy
by Frederica Mathewes-Green
San Francisco: Harper Collins Pub., 1997.
https://www.amazon.com/Facing-East-Pilgrims-Mysteries-Orthodoxy/dp/0060850000/

Byzantine Theology
by John Meyendorff
NY: Fordham University Press, 1979.
https://www.amazon.com/Byzantine-Theology-Historical-Trends-Doctrinal/dp/0823209679/

Interpreting Orthodoxy: The Communication of Eastern Orthodox Beliefs to Christians of Western Church Traditions
by Dr. N. A Nissiotis
Minneapolis: Light and Life Publishing Co.
https://www.amazon.com/Interpreting-Orthodoxy-Dr-N-Nissiotis/dp/B001J1U2SE

The Christian Tradition: A History of the Development of Doctrine, Volume 2, The Spirit of Eastern Christendom (600-1700)
by Jaroslav Pelikan
Chicago: University of Chicago Press, 1977.
https://www.amazon.com/Christian-Tradition-Development-Doctrine-Christendom/dp/0226653730

Introduction to Liturgical Theology,
by Alexander Schmemann transl. Ashleigh Moorehouse
Crestwood, NY: St. Vladimir's Seminary Press, 1975.
https://www.amazon.com/Introduction-Liturgical-Theology-Alexander-Schmemann/dp/0913836184/

The Eucharist
by Alexander Schmemann transl. Paul Kachur
Crestwood, NY: St. Vladimir's Seminary Press, 1988.
https://www.amazon.com/Eucharist-Sacrament-Kingdom-Alexander-Schmemann/dp/0881410187/

For the Life of the World: Sacraments and Orthodoxy
by Alexander Schmemann
Crestwood, NY: St. Vladimir's Seminary Press, 1988.
https://www.amazon.com/Life-World-Sacraments-Orthodoxy/dp/0913836087/

The Deification of Man
by Liadain Sherrard, transl., Georgios I. Mantzaridis,
NY: St Vladimir's Seminary Press, 1984.
https://www.amazon.com/Deification-Man-Tradition-Contemporary-Theologians/dp/0881410276

The Law of God
by Seraphim Slobodskoy
NY: Holy Trinity Monastery, 1994.
http://bookstore.jordanville.org/9780884650447

In the Spirit of Happiness
by The Monks of New Skete,
Boston: Little, Brown & Co., 1999.
https://www.amazon.com/Spirit-Happiness-Monks-New-Skete/dp/0316606944/

The Orthodox Church
by Timothy (Fr. Kallistos) Ware
London: Penguin Press, 1993.
http://www.amazon.com/Orthodox-Church-New-Timothy-Ware/dp/0140146563

The Orthodox Way
by Fr. Kallistos Ware
Crestwood, NY: St. Vladimir's Seminary Press, 1986.
https://www.amazon.com/Orthodox-Way-Kallistos-Ware/dp/0913836583/

The Philokalia: The Complete Text (Vol. 1)
Compiled by St. Nikodimos of the Holy Mountain and St. Markarios of Corinth
by G. E.H. Palmer (Translator), Philip Sherrard (Translator), Kallistos Ware
Faber & Faber, January 1, 1983
https://www.amazon.com/Philokalia-Complete-Compiled-Nikodimos-Markarios/dp/0571130135/

Online Reading and Resources

FaithEncouraged.org
Faith Encouraged Ministries - Daily devotionals and other writings
www.faithencouraged.org

Origins of the Divine Liturgy (online resource)
http://www.goarch.org/ourfaith/ourfaith7117

Fr John Breck- Reflections on the Bible and liturgy (online resource)
https://oca.org/reflections/fr.-john-breck/bible-and-liturgy

Human Person as a Being Created in the Image of God and as the Image of the Son: The Orthodox Christian Perspective (online essay)
by Prof. Nicolae Razvan Stan
http://orthodox-theology.com/media/PDF/IJOT3-2011/Stan-Human.pdf

Wisdom in the Orthodox Faith (online essay)
https://oca.org/orthodoxy/the-orthodox-faith/spirituality/the-virtues/wisdom1

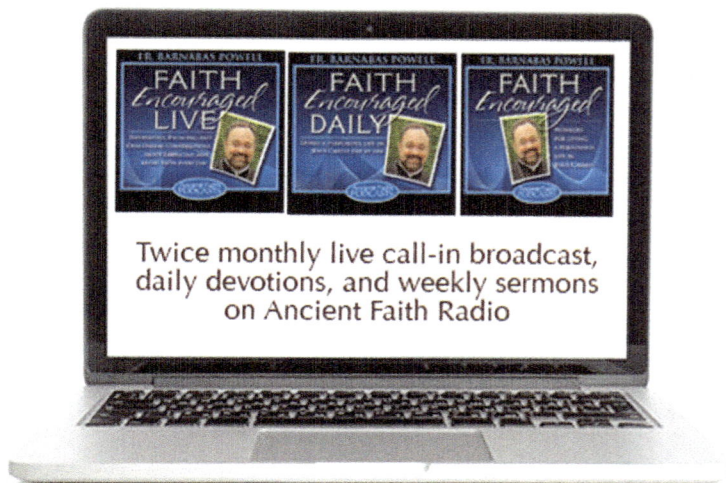

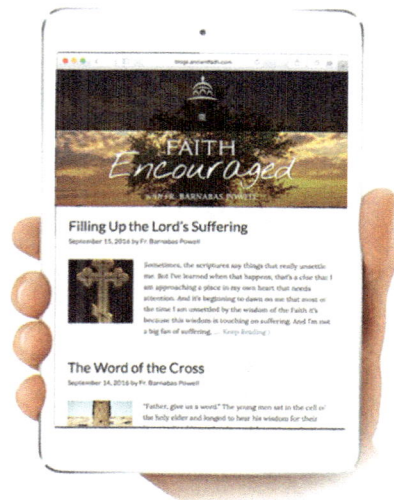

89

CPSIA information can be obtained
at www.ICGtesting.com
Printed in the USA
LVOW05s1942161216
517647LV00002B/2/P

9 781944 967147